The Man Who
Dropped the Le Creuset
on His Toe
and Other Bourgeois Mishaps

Also by Christopher Matthew

A Different World: Stories of Great Hotels
The Long-Haired Boy
Three Men in a Boat (annotated edition with Benny Green)
The Junket Man
How to Survive Middle Age
The Amber Room
A Nightingale Sang in Fernhurst Road
Now We Are Sixty
Now We Are Sixty (and a Bit)
Summoned by Balls
When We Were Fifty

The Simon Crisp Diaries:

Diary of a Somebody
Loosely Engaged
The Crisp Report
Family Matters
Knocking On

The Man Who Dropped the Le Creuset on His Toe

and Other Bourgeois Mishaps

CHRISTOPHER MATTHEW

Illustrations by Tony Ross

Little, Brown

LITTLE, BROWN

First published in Great Britain in 2013 by Little, Brown
Reprinted 2013 (twice)

A CIP catalogue record for this book
is available from the British Library.

ISBN 978-1-40870-465-3

Designed and typeset in Kingfisher by Geoff Green Book Design
Printed and bound in Great Britain by
Clays Ltd, St Ives plc

Papers used by Little, Brown are from well-managed forests
and other responsible sources.

MIX
Paper from
responsible sources
FSC
www.fsc.org   FSC® C104740

Little, Brown
An imprint of
Little, Brown Book Group
100 Victoria Embankment
London EC4Y 0DY

An Hachette UK Company
www.hachette.co.uk

www.littlebrown.co.uk

To all of those for whom life has a nasty habit of
suddenly turning round and biting them in the leg.

Contents

Contents

Introduction

Accidents are nearly always idiotic, and sometimes positively bizarre. Normally unavoidable, they catch even the wariest of us at the most unlikely moments. However sensibly, or intelligently, or carefully we pick our way through the hither and yon of daily life, something is often waiting to bring us up in our tracks – be it the lamp-post one walks into while looking the other way, the garden rake that lies upright, waiting for the misplaced boot, or the panic attack that induces the normally level-headed men to curtsey to the Duke of Edinburgh.

P. G. Wodehouse put it down to pure fate, which, 'if it slips us a bit of goose with one hand, is pretty sure to give us the sleeve across the windpipe with the other.'

The English middle classes are, on the whole, treated to more good luck than most. Indeed, they often feel it to be their entitlement; so that when something unexpected happens to shake them out of their routine of complacency, it comes as a much greater shock than it might to those for whom life is altogether more grim and earnest.

I have still to recover from the moment in March 2010 when, having eased myself out of a chair lift in a Swiss ski resort – something I had been doing man and boy without any problems for over sixty years – I stumbled, fell sideways into a pile of snow and broke my hip.

Undergoing the operation (while awake, I might say), spending weeks with crutches, a walking stick and physiotherapy wasn't half as much fun as telling people about it. The more I told the story, the more I embellished it, until it began to take on the semblance – not to say the length – of a stand-up routine at the Hammersmith Apollo.

People enjoy hearing about other people's accidents – the more exotic and idiotic the better. Those who have had a similar experience are relieved to know they are not alone; those who have not are happy in their mistaken assumption that nothing as silly as that can happen to them.

I myself experienced this blissful sense of *schadenfreude* when describing my hip adventures to my editor, Richard Beswick, and he, having listened sympathetically, announced that he had recently dropped a Le Creuset casserole on his toe.

I didn't mean to laugh. In fact, my first reaction was to wince. However, the name Le Creuset added unexpected humour to the story – quite undeserved on Richard's part, since his toe was beginning to turn black and he would probably lose the nail, if not the entire toe.

On the other hand, the inclusion of the brand name immediately summed up the world in which cast-iron casseroles and other expensive kitchenware are part of the everyday landscape, and their owners should know better than to drop them on their toes. It was a classic bourgeois mishap, or middle-class disaster.

So too, I hope, are the cock-ups, catastrophes, calamities

and cataclysms described in the collection of comic, if at times wince-making, verses contained in this slim volume.

Some really happened to people I know, others to people who know the people they happened to, and some are just plain made up.

And, since you ask, my hip is better than it was, but still a bit stiff after I've been sitting. Like now, for example.

Christopher Matthew
London, November 2013

The Man Who
Dropped the Le Creuset
on His Toe

and Other Bourgeois Mishaps

Trolleyed

Grizelda was a happy soul,
As kind as she was jolly,
Until the day she lost control,
Pushing a Waitrose trolley.

She shot between the fruit and veg,
Like someone on the Cresta
Aboard a disobedient sledge.
This all took place in Leicester.

Competitive Dad

A prat-in-chief was Charlie Plank –
A fellow born to brag and swank.
But worse still was his urge to win
Against his junior kith and kin.
Whatever any child could do,
He'd prove that he could do it, too –
And not just do it, do it better
In Lycra shorts or chunky sweater.

By his account, he was a man
Who'd been a true Olympian.
In his time he had faced the best
(Including Seb Coe in a vest).
He'd fenced at Cambridge, boxed there too,
And would have got a rowing blue,
But caught a crab just near Barnes Bridge
When bitten by a giant midge,
And lost his place to dear old Hugh
(That friend of Stephen You Know Who),
A story he was very fond
Of telling at the boating pond,
Where not one child could win a race
With Daddy rowing at full pace.

He'd make his youngest look a fool
In swimming galas at the pool
By seemingly to be all heart
And giving him a ten-yard start,
Then underlining adult strength
By thrashing him by half a length.

He really was a frightful pill;
He'd beat all three by thirty nil
In soccer contests in the park
That dragged on well into the dark.
His batting skills were in no doubt;
He once made two-two-eight not out.

There was one sport where they excelled:
Their skiing was unparalleled –
The simple reason being they
Had started young in old Saas-Fee;
And being so close to the snow
They'd ski as fast as they could go.
Not having very far to fall,
They hadn't any fear at all.

Now Charles was nearly thirty-eight
When he had learnt to ski (and skate) –
The same time as his cool young brood,
Though in a slightly grumpy mood
When relegated to a group
Of older types – a cautious troupe
Who took their time with gentle turns
And lots of cream on lots of burns.

Still, Charlie saw no reason why
He should not keep up with his fry;
So, after lunch (and full of wine)
He'd set off with the little swine.
The faster that they went, he'd go
Careering wildly through the snow,
Determined to be at the front,
Despite the odd disastrous shunt
That left him sprawling on his face –
A faller in snow's steeplechase.

One day while heading off to lunch,
They happened on a cheerful bunch
Of local children doing jumps
On fairly simple, rough-hewn bumps,
And, dauntless in the frosty air,
Were showing off their freestyle flair
With flips and twists and spins and kicks,
Plus several ad hoc hotdog tricks.

The boys could only stand and stare;
They knew that they could never dare
To beat the locals at their game,
And Dad, of course, was far too lame ...

'Wow! That looks fun!' they hear him cry.
'Come on, chaps, let's all have a try!'
They hang their heads and look away;
Next thing they know, he's under way,
With legs spread wide and arms akimbo,
Their father's floating by in limbo ...

He broke his hip, his pelvis too,
A tibia, a rib or two,
And, helmetless, he bashed his head,
And, sad to say, he's now stone dead.

A gravestone tells the sorry tale
Of this most tragic alpha male.
It's written there beneath his name:
WHATE'ER THE ODDS, HE WON THE GAME.

The Shaming of Anthea Sims

Our pub quiz team is one bod short
Since Anthea Sims was one day caught
Alone inside the ladies' loo
In serious chat with who knows who,
With BlackBerry attached to ear
And whispering, 'I can't quite hear.
Was that Leif Ericson you said,
The son of whatsisname, The Red?'

When challenged by the opposition,
She claimed a mild indisposition.
'I've had some trouble with my bowels,'
She said in well-bred, cut-glass vowels.
'I wouldn't want it spread around;
You know how things like this rebound.
Next thing I'll hear I'm at death's door!
I didn't want to be a bore;
I thought I'd ring the surgery ...
I swear this isn't perjury ...
My doctor's name is Ericson,
Which, as you know, means Eric's son ...
His father was a Communist,
A well-known gynaecologist,
Known fondly as "The Red" by mums,
And some of us have stayed good chums ...
He's ninety now and very spry,
And living on the Isle of Skye ...

She rambled on, but all in vain;
She sounded more and more insane.
The game was up; she knew it, too.
There was nothing she could do
But stand there as if in a trance;
She wouldn't get a second chance.

She had to go; she knew the rules;
She couldn't take us *all* for fools.

Her eyes welled up; she shed a tear;
She didn't stop to drink her beer;
She stumbled out, sad sight indeed –
A salted snail in oatmeal tweed.

We haven't won a quiz night since;
Our scores would make a schoolboy wince;
While Anthea, you'll be pleased to find,
Is doing well on *Mastermind* –
At home, with all her reference books,
And no one there to give dark looks.

Builders' Last Laugh

I've got this foreign builder chap,
A nice young man called Fred.
I can't tell by his accent,
But I think he's quite well bred.

We always have a lot of laughs;
He's now a kind of friend.
He couldn't be more helpful, but
He drives me round the bend.

I bought some instant Carte Noire
(From Waitrose, since you ask:
I challenge anyone to say
I cannot multi-task.)

One does one's best to get on terms
With builders and the like,
But ... well ... as far as they're concerned,
We lot can take a hike.

He never even touched the stuff,
Preferring, so I glean,
Nespresso macchiato
From our spanking new machine.

I didn't like to mention it;
One doesn't like to fuss.
One's dealings with one's builders
Are invariably thus.

Last week I came home early and
There, slumbering in our bed
Was Joachim the plasterer,
And, next to him, young Fred.

Tragedia Toscana

The doyens of Chiantishire
Were Jill and Johnny Uthwatt-Burr.
The couple had a yen to roam,
But Tuscany's their home from home –
To be precise, near Montalcino,
Where they enjoyed an annual beano
Of gastro outings there and here
To recommended *trattorie*.

The five-star choice in all the books
Was owned by Aldo – 'Cook of Cooks'.
Il Gamberetto was its name,
And such its fast-expanding fame
That it could take three months or more
To get one's foot inside the door.

The Uthwatt-Burrs pulled every string,
But nothing that they did could swing
A booking on their last night there.
Dear God! They simply couldn't bear
To think of eating *en famille*
Instead of one last gastro spree.

But good will come to those who wait,
And shortly after ten to eight
A man called from the restaurant
To say that if they came along,
A cock-up by the *maître d'*
Had left a corner table free.

The couple didn't pause to think;
They chucked the meat sauce in the sink,
And sprinted to the hired Fiat,
Triumphant that at last they'd be at
One of *the* great seafood joints,
Which in their foodie eyes meant POINTS.

John gave the little car full power
And got there in just half an hour ...

The Soave vanished down their gullets;
The waiter brought their grilled red mullets.
John smacked his lips; he took a bite.
Jill's eyes popped out; her face turned white.
She said, 'Oh bollocks! What an ass!
I've left our pasta on the gas!'

The walls turned black, the gas stove burst.
At least they ate their dinner first.

Boden Man

Zak's father, hot and sweaty,
In cargo shorts and specs,
Leapt smugly off a jetty,
Displaying well-formed pecs.

They found him quite soon after;
'Oh no!' they heard him shout.
He couldn't have looked dafter;
The ruddy tide was out.

Boogie Frights

Elizabeth and Rupert Gore
Were magic on the ballroom floor.
The quickstep was their claim to fame:
Unbeatable when on their game,
They'd won some prizes as a pair
At local dances here and there.
In Spain they cleaned up with a tango,
Which shows the way that these things can go.

Once, on a cruise, they cut a rug
And triumphed with a jitterbug,
And concentrated thence on disco –
A skill they honed in San Francisco.
Their *pièce de* was gangnam style:
They stood out by a country mile
From amateurs who 'did their thing',
With all the tripe that that can bring.

At forty-five they hit their peak
In Haslemere in Easter Week
At Boo and Henry's wedding bash,
Where, after dins, they cut a dash
So lively that the bride and groom
(And virtually half the room)
Stood there in silence, mouths ajar,
Like pop fans with a superstar.

Two teenagers were standing near;
One said out loud, so all could hear,
'It's sad to see the elderly
Pretending to be you and me.
If only they would act their age.
They're too old to take centre stage.'

They never hit the floor again
In England, France, or on the main.
These days they live in Argentina
(A much more tolerant arena),
And tango till their arches fall,
And no one laughs at them at all.

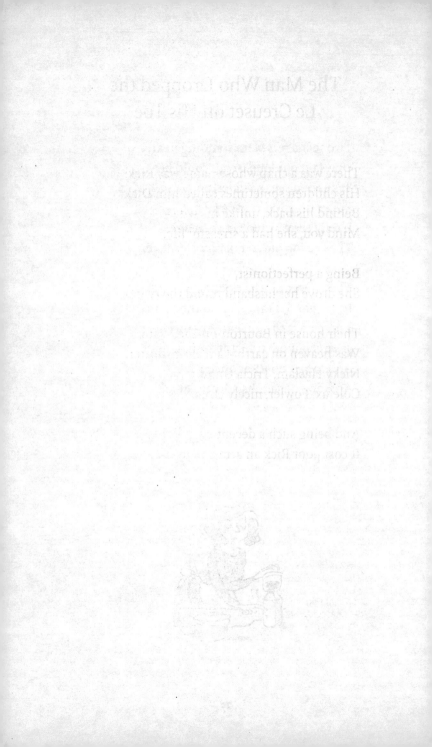

The Man Who Dropped the Le Creuset on His Toe

There was a chap whose name was Rick;
His children sometimes called him Dick
Behind his back, unlike his wife –
Mind you, she had a stressful life.

Being a perfectionist,
She drove her husband round the twist.

Their house in Bourton-on-the-Water
Was heaven on earth – a real ripsnorter.
Nicky Haslam, Tricia Guild,
Colefax, Fowler, nicely chilled,

And being such a decent egg,
It cost poor Rick an arm and leg.

Her kitchen was her pride and joy:
Equipped with every trick and toy,
It had a cosy farmhouse look –
A rocking chair, an inglenook,
And just a hint of sex appeal
With fabrics dyed in cochineal,
And every surface clean and bare –
No sign of clutter anywhere.

Her maxim was that less means more;
Hence every cupboard, every drawer
Was filled with trendy kitchenware
Of every shape and size, I swear.
And some you wouldn't think exist –
Not even on a wedding list.

An Eva Solo Citrus Squeezer;
Zabaglione pans from Pisa;
Alessi electronic scales;
Nantucket Seafood plates for snails;

A set of Kai Wasabi knives;
A small machine for chopping chives;
A Jasper Conran salad bowl –
A hoard of gastro rock 'n' roll.

Now Rick was quite a helpful chap,
And when he thought the time was ripe,
He'd do a spot of washing up,
But chances were he'd break a cup.

He'd undertake the simplest task;
He wouldn't say, he'd never ask,
And sent his wife completely mad;
His kids would smirk and murmur 'Da-a-ad.'

Undaunted, he would drive her gaga
By cooking on the gas-fired Aga.
One day he tried a Sunday roast –
The poor lamb ended up as toast.

His wife in desperation banned
Him from the kitchen, raised her hand
And said (with quite unusual force),
'One more false move and it's divorce!'

But Rick was not a man to quail,
Or wail, or pale, or rail, or fail.
He'd give his wife a nice surprise,
And be a hero in her eyes.

A stew, he felt, would hit the spot –
A simple dish, but good and hot,
With meat and veg and spuds and wine –
A blend of Oliver and Stein,

With just a hint of Eastern spice –
The sort Koreans find quite nice.
A *tang* perhaps, or maybe *guk*,
As per her Eastern cookery book.

He settled on a dish from Seoul
And fetched the biggest casserole –
Volcanic red by You-Know-Who,
Cast iron, natch, for perfect stew.

He grabs Le Creuset with both hands,
He trips, it falls, and promptly lands –
Oh, wretched fate; oh, cruel blow –
Slap, bang upon his big right toe.

The nail went black, infection came.
He said, 'I'm really not to blame.'
The children groaned, 'You shouldn't try, Dad.'
His life was one long jeremiad;
And when he had his toe removed,
His wife was, frankly, quite unmoved.
She said, 'Well, what can you expect?
You have no skills in this respect.
Mind you, it worked out on the whole;
You could have smashed the Conran bowl.'

Belinda Brown, Who Logged Out in No Uncertain Terms

Belinda Brown was no one's fool –
The brightest of the bright at school;
A polymath of deep conviction,
And yet a well of contradiction.
The owner of a doctorate;
Computer-wise – illiterate.

For reasons she could not explain,
She bought a ticket (to Bahrain) –
Not through her travel agent, Brett,
But online via the internet.
Again, for reasons inexplicable,
She filled in something inapplicable.
Convinced she'd failed, she tried once more,
And now was absolutely sure
She'd coughed up twice. *But how to check?*
It drove her mad, she was a wreck.

A nervous breakdown followed fast;
The trouble was, it never passed.
And now she lives in North Tibet,
Enraptured by the internet

Arrest Ye Merry

Tom Balls was a contrarian –
A smooth-faced, yet quite hairy man.
Religion was a case in point;
His faith was badly out of joint.
In empty churches quite devout,
In full ones much beset by doubt.
But once a year on Christmas Eve
He did his utmost to believe,
Upon his knees around midnight,
Comforted by candlelight.

But hard as Thomas tried to pray,
Attention would too often stray.

One Christmas, hot foot from the pub
(And feeling, frankly, somewhat sub),
Tom casually glanced along the pew
And saw a blonde girl dressed in blue,
Who bore a likeness, very slightly,
To Tom's great heart throb, Keira Knightley.

While murmuring the Gloria,
Transported by euphoria,
He stole a glance. She looked straight back.
He nearly had a cardiac.
She smiled. He felt his face go red.
Instead of God, he thought of bed,
And, at the altar on cloud nine,
He swallowed half a cup of wine.

His legs were weak; his arms the same;
His head was light; he felt no shame.
He stumbled back along the aisle,
His face fixed in a silly smile.
He knelt and bowed his head in prayer:
'Dear Lord,' he said, 'I know you're fair.
You don't do deals, I know that much,
And this is not an ask, as such,
But one kind word from Keira there,
And I'll rejoin the fold, I swear.'

He mingled with the crowd outside,
While trying to look dignified,
But of the girl there was no sign.
He had a word with Caroline,
The vicar, and drove home to bed,
Rather wishing he was dead.

He hadn't travelled very far
When, flagged down by a panda car,
He failed a breathalyser test,
And felt decidedly unblessed.

He's not first man to be shocked
That God is never lightly mocked.

Mary, Who Gave Up Well-Tuned Glutes
for Well-Turned Prose

One way to cure a wobbly arse
Is join a small Pilates class.
It sorts your abs, your hips, your thighs,
And frequently can lower size
From eighteen-plus to under ten,
And make you feel yourself again.

Now Mary Slim (ill-suited name
For such a fatty, such a shame)
Each Tuesday morning, fresh and bright
(With joints and muscles fairly tight),
Would take her mat and pink toe socks,
Her water and three lightweight blocks,
And rush off to the local gym
To shake a leg and stretch a limb
On Tower Trainer, Cadillac
And Ladder Barrel (brown and black).
Then, following this weekly grind,
She'd join her ladies and unwind
With skinny lattes, herbal teas,
And chew the fat and shoot the breeze.

But long, lean legs and firm, flat tum,
And well-toned abs and slinky bum
Were not to be for Mary Slim.
Her life, for her, was looking grim.
Despite her efforts on the mat,
She stayed unwaveringly fat.

Her spirits drooped, her midriff too.
'Why can't I do what others do?'
She wailed. 'My pelvis and my spine
Are nicely flexed and well in line,
But, bum-wise, I'm still Rubenesque –
A freak of nature, a grotesque.'

'I like you just the way you are,'
Her husband told her in the car.
'To tell the truth, these pecs and abs
Give me the serious abdabs.'

But no girl can be satisfied
Whose bottom measures six feet wide,
When all their fellow Pilatees
Are Katie Moss-like, if you please.

Now Mary was like one possessed
(Though keep-fit types are all obsessed).
She bought her own Deluxe Trapeze
And went at it like Herakles
Against the lion of Nemea,
Without an ounce of doubt or fear.

But, sad to say, this lion won,
And Mary at long last was done.
Her bum was her Achilles heel;
Though how it brought her down, I feel,
I'd rather not divulge right now;
Suffice to say, a pregnant cow
Could not have made a louder din
Than Mary, when they took her in;
And nurses of huge strength and skill
With training from Stoke Mandeville
Spent ages trying to untangle
Poor Mary's limbs from every angle.

She sold all her Pilates gear,
Half price, to Di who lived quite near,
And joined a local reading group –
A cosy, unambitious troupe,
For whom the latest P. D. James
Is worth a million slim-tone frames.

Chilling Out

A long weekend in Devon
For Julian and Fee
Was somewhat less than heaven,
They couldn't but agree.

The hotel was perfection,
The food the best by far;
But a serious objection
Was the rubbish mini-bar.

A nightcap after dinner
Would end a magic day;
But all that they had in there
Was a middling Chardonnay.

Basket Case

A pompous man was 'Sunny' Jim,
And, frankly, he was rather dim.
Four undistinguished years at Stowe
Meant he had nowhere else to go
But in the Church or in a bank,
Or in the army in a tank.
In fact, he had a dull career:
A humdrum Royal Engineer.
A major, it is true to say,
But not a type who made his way.
A decade's worth of selling soap
Had followed, but with little hope
Of making something of his life,
Or landing a half-decent wife.

And so he'd spent his latter years
Annoying people, bending ears,
Correcting grammar, picking holes
In politicians, scoring goals
In pointless, idiotic fights
With parking wardens, Labourites,
Nice ladies with their lollipops,
Young men with shaven heads in shops.
The tiniest whisper of a scrap,
He'd find it hard to shut his trap.
He'd argue morning, noon and night,
Convinced that he was always right.

For him there was no greater crime
Than wasting energy and time
In cluttered aisles and checkout lines
Of twerpish, half-baked philistines –
Their trolleys piled with special deals
On Heinz baked beans and ten-quid meals.
He'd fill a basket with the speed
Of starlings on a field of seed,
Then head unerringly for where
The shortest queue was he could bear.
One in particular he'd choose
(Except when stocking up with booze),
Reserved for those with special need –
i.e. a single mouth to feed.
One day he found himself alone
With perky checkout lady, Joan.
He counted out his meagre fare;
The sign above was clear as clear.

'A loaf of multi-seeded bread;
A mini-jar of salmon spread;
A guacamole dip (one scoop);
A tin of cock-a-leekie soup;
A dozen eggs. Five items, yes?
No problem there. No sweat. No stress.'
He dropped his voice to sound benign
And pointed upwards at the sign –
'Misuse of English gets my goat;
Forgive me, just a tiny note:
Merely a matter of finesse,
It should read FEWER there, not LESS.'

The checkout girl said, 'Thank you, sir.
I'd be quite happy to concur,
Except you've got six items here.
You've chosen the wrong queue, I fear.'

Her colleague came; a row broke out;
And Jim, as per, began to shout.
The manager was very nice:
'Two boxes of six eggs count twice,'
He said. 'The best thing you can do
Is join a proper, full-length queue.'

An hour later Jim emerged,
His sense of outrage still unpurged,
And set off in the murk and damp
To find his car had got a clamp.

Now coronaries can change a chap
As quickly as a thunderclap;
And Jim lay calmly on the ground
While paramedics bustled round.
A stoic air suffused his face
As IV lines were put in place,
And reassuring things were said,
And pillows placed around his head.
But Jim was made of sterner stuff,
And very soon he'd had enough
Of soothing words so kindly meant,
And helping hands so kindly lent.
He said, 'I've got one bone to pick:
These traffic wardens made me sick.
For years I've tried, God knows I've tried ...'
And with those words the poor chap died –
Brave-hearted warrior to the end,
And never short of ears to bend.

Underachievement

I'm a fan of Mountbatten of Burma,
But I wish I'd been Paddy Leigh Fermor.
I'm a handy old sod
If I'm given the nod,
But I'm stuck here in dull *terra firma*.

The Lead in the Boxing Glove

In Chipping Forelock, Oxfordshire,
The biggest cheese was Jimbo Spurr.
A parish councillor for years,
He held his own among his peers.
A small man (like his hero Proust) –
His dear wife Margie ran the roost;
But in the village he stood tall,
Like Caesar when he'd conquered Gaul.

But all too often Fate will shove
The lead into the boxing glove,
And great men will come crashing down,
Like Pagliaccio – poor clown.

One night, while in the Land of Nod,
The phone went. Jimbo said, 'Dear God!
Who can that be at half-past two?
Hello? Who's that? You what? To who?
I've never heard of such a thing!
Electric dungeon? Penis ring?
You must be mad. Oh, here's my wife.
I think *you* need to get a life.'

Now Margie was no silly prude,
But what she heard was, frankly, rude.
'Disgusting!' was her brisk retort.
'Good night,' she added with a snort.

Next night the same man rang again,
And several more in search of pain.
Night after night the calls poured in;
The Spurrs just took them on the chin.
But lack of sleep can take its toll
And Margie lost her self-control.
She said, 'If you don't sort this out,
I swear I'm going walkabout!'

Then Jimbo had a bright idea:
'It's not because they want *you*, dear.
Let's face it, it's not quite your bag.
An advert in a porno mag
Has used our number by mistake,
And hence your current bellyache.
I'm popping out. I shan't be long.
I'll see if I can right this wrong.'

He hurried to the village shop,
Where, like an undercover cop,
He scanned the shelves of magazines –
The *Vogue*s, the *Harper's*, and the *Queen*s.
His eyes looked up and there above
Were all the boobs and bums men love.

He looked around, the place was clear;
The owner, George, was nowhere near.
He stretched an arm, he seized *Big Tits*
And held it in his trembling mitts.
He opened up and riffled through;
His eyes popped out, his brain thought, Phew!

A voice said, 'Can I help you, sir?'
What followed next was all a blur.
George wore a silly, knowing grin,
And standing by a Mars bar bin
Was Trish, a local magistrate,
And one of Forelock's good and great.

Poor Jimbo's face had turned bright red.
The next thing was, he lost his head.
'This isn't what it might appear.
I'm looking for a number here.
It's not my fault. There's been a mess.
And someone's put the wrong address ...'

He gabbled on, and coughed and spluttered;
George nodded sagely, then he muttered,
'I understand, sir. Say no more.'
For Trish this was the final straw.
She shook her head and rolled her eyes;
Her feelings she could not disguise.

The last they heard of Jimbo Spurr,
He'd moved to north Carmarthenshire,
Where Margie runs a B&B,
And Jimbo makes the morning tea.
And no men ring at half-past two
To tell them what they'd like to do.

Nouveaux Pauvres

Susie and Nick are feeling sick –
The bank has rung warning bells.
Next year they may be forced to pick
Zermatt *or* the Seychelles.

Weekenders

When Don and James set off for Gwent
To weekend in the place they rent,
It takes an hour to pack the car.
The front step looks like a bazaar,
With Waitrose bags and crates of wine,
And tennis racquets, tied with twine,
A holdall full of windsurf gear,
Assorted plants, six-packs of beer,
Clean laundry from their previous stay,
And board games that they rarely play,
The dog's cage, biscuits, squeaky toys,
A pair of Don's old corduroys
To make the poor mutt feel at home,
Her bowl, her mat, her treats, her comb,
Her grooming brush, her cans and pouches –
They pack the lot, they are no slouches.
Compared with Pickfords at their best,
In packing terms, there's no contest.

From Holland Park to Ebbw Vale
(In Gwent) takes, via hill and dale,
Around three hours, give or take –
About right for a weekend break,
Depending on what time they leave.
To chance one's arm is plain naïve.
The boys are usually on their way
By eight a.m. on Saturday –
Though if their diaries are just right,
They'll get away on Friday night.

To watch them load their old hatchback
Is like that old-time circus act
When twenty clowns would fill a car
No bigger than a Kilner jar.

Beginning with the food and booze,
Enough to last a ten-day cruise,
They fill up every nook and cranny,
Their spatial skills are quite uncanny.
And on the back seat, to the right,
Behind the driver, out of sight,
There's room for one small cashmere rug –
The perfect spot for one small pug.

Bambina's their beloved's name;
It's seven years since madam came
Into their lives – their would-be child,
A loving daughter, sweet and mild.
There's nothing those two wouldn't do
To please their little Bubsy-Boo.

One Friday evening, South Wales-bound,
Near Wootton Bassett, Don turned round
To have a word with little Boo –
'Hello, there, sweetheart. How are you?'

He leant across, gave her a pat;
The rug was there, but that was that.

'Bambina, darling? Bloody hell …!
Where is she?' He'd begun to yell.

'You're joking!' James let out a groan.
The pair were both completely thrown.
He parked the car; they both got out;
He peered inside; there was no doubt.
Of Bubsy there was not a sign.
An icy chill ran down his spine.

The accusations ebbed and flowed
Across the middle of the road.
Both thought the other was to blame,
But it was just a pointless game.
The fact remained that they were there
And Bubsy-Boo was quite elsewhere.

They called each other twerps and prats,
And screeched like two Kilkenny cats
The whole way down the motorway,
With frequent breaks to groan and pray.

They came at last to Holland Park,
And on the pavement in the dark
Sat Bubsy-Boo, cucumber cool.
Unlike those two, she was no fool.

With shrieks of joy and boo-hoo-hoo,
They fell upon their Bubsy-Boo,
Who viewed them both with deep disdain,
Like Eleanor of Aquitaine
When, bored with Louis, King of France,
She booted him and took a chance
On Henry, Duke of Normandy,
Of far superior pedigree.

The humbler the pie they ate,
The less did she appreciate
Their treats, their toys, their coos, their hugs –
The little things that humour pugs.

If dogs could turn their noses up,
She would have won a silver cup.

They never went to Wales again;
The very thought caused too much pain.
Their partnership began to crack;
One day Don dealt his friend a smack.
Confused, Boo gave a high-pitched cry,
And sank her teeth into his thigh.

So, after that, she had to go –
To friends who lived in Pimlico,
And had a seaside house in Kent
Which Bubsy loved much more than Gwent.

And James and Don are now divorced.
It's no one's fault; they were not forced.
But, face it, no home's quite so sweet
Without a dog around your feet.

Caught on Camera

Achilles de Gray's a big cheese in PR,
Who enjoys all life's bounteous rewards.
He's a bit of a love-rat, as some types are,
And each year takes a large box at Lord's.

He invites lots of people he doesn't know well:
Mainly clients in showbiz and stuff,
And a chap called Roberto – a maître d'hotel –
And his boyfriend, a nice bit of rough.

He prefers it if everyone sits in full view
Of the spies in the Media Centre,
Where they may well be spotted by who-knows-who,
And picked out by a TV presenter.

He sits there himself, well exposed, in the middle,
One hand round a glass of champagne,
Getting up only when in dire need of a widdle,
Or to speak to his secretary, Jane.

One day he returned, feeling duly revived,
And a ghastly pain shot through his arse.
He leapt to his feet and found he'd contrived
To sit slap on his own champagne glass.

He yelled and he swore like the old Minotaur
As he tried to assess the damage.
He wasn't concerned with the pain: it was more
To do with his undercarriage.

And as Jane rubbed his bum with a soothing palm,
And smothered his face with kisses,
And cuddled him tight with a loving arm,
It was clear she could show him what bliss is ...

He twisted and turned and wriggled his hips
Like a Bollywood dancer in Delhi,
As his wife watched it all with well-pursed lips
On the screen of their drawing-room telly.

The Woman Who Found Her Arms Were Too Short

A bugbear for Amanda Mears
Was driving cars with manual gears.
At twenty she would lurch and hop,
Surprised to find herself in top.
She'd try to force the damned thing in
And make the most appalling din.
Her husband, Matt, would sigh and moan,
Like Mistrals blowing down the Rhone.
'For God's sake, woman, sort them out;
They're all in the same box,' he'd shout.

The day she bought an automatic
Her driving was far less erratic,
And thoughts of imminent divorce
Were soon replaced by true remorse.

Amanda, growing quite blasé,
Once popped to Brighton for the day
With Milly from next door but one,
And Maggot, who was rather fun.
The sun was shining as she wove
Her way along the coast to Hove,
And turned into a multi-storey,
Feeling pretty hunky-dory –
Until she reached the ticket thing
And found that she was struggling
To stretch her right arm out that far –
At least while sitting in the car.

'Oh dear,' she said, 'I never thought
My arms were really quite so short.
Don't move, you two; you stay right here.'

Forgetting she was still in gear,
She swung the door and stepped outside
And seized the ticket, arms spread wide,
In time to see the car proceed
At what one might call stately speed
Into the barrier and beyond,
Quite like a swan upon a pond.

It struck a Porsche and then a Merc,
And after that it got to work
On several brand new motorbikes,
A Golf, an Audi and the likes,
And came to rest against a wall –
As if after a road-rage brawl.

The damage stood at fifty thou,
And no one could explain just how
A clever woman without peer
Could not quite get her brain in gear.

Hallelujah

Ptolemy Smith has a lovely voice
(A lightish baritone by choice),
And recently he gave his all
With thousands at the Albert Hall,
Who pack it for the Scratch *Messiah* –
A massively ebullient choir.

His host, a breezy golfing chum,
Was very keen that he should come –
'For us it's just a bit of fun;
A good old sing-song, no harm done!
There's no rehearsal, no run-through,
And, frankly, we don't have a clue!'

But Ptolemy was no cheap slouch,
As friends and family will vouch.
He treats things like this seriously,
Declaring quite imperiously,
'One cannot take old Handel lightly;
He's thought to be the best – and rightly.'

So, every night for weeks ahead,
He mugged up on the score in bed,
Until he knew it off by heart –
At least, the baritone's main part.

But on the day a croaky throat
Produced the odd high croaky note,
So on the way he stopped and bought
A miniature of top class port
(A well-known recipe for pros,
As once prescribed by Berlioz),
And, pausing at the entrance door,
He took a swig and then some more ...

The wine began to warm and soothe;
His tonsils turned from rough to smooth,
And, like a carefree meadowlark
Ascending in a glorious arc,
His spirit soared, his voice burst free;
He warbled loud enough for three.

His jokey pals were most impressed
By Ptolemy's unbounded zest –
Though less so at the very end
When seven thousand loud 'Amen'-ed,
And, as the silence filled the hall
Before the last 'Amen' of all,
One voice rang out – a baritone
'Amen'-ing proudly on its own.

The golfers thought it quite a joke
And said, 'You *really* went for broke!
Why, anyone out there would think
That someone was the worse for drink!'

His friends now call him Pavarotti;
The poor chap's nearly going potty.

Georgina,
the Socialite Who Went to Pot

Georgina was a party girl;
Her life was one long social whirl.
At smart occasions every week
She'd meet the most exclusive clique
Of well-known names and lords and earls,
Good-looking men and pretty girls,
Assorted entries in *Who's Who* –
All generally well-to-do.

So dinner parties held no fears,
Not after thirty-seven years.
Polite, amusing and well-dressed,
She was the perfect party guest.
But then one day she lost her head,
And, frankly, wished that she was dead.

Pre-dinner with her best friend, Sybil,
A most delicious type of nibble
Stood near her in a flowery pot –
She very nearly ate the lot,
Until a fellow from Missouri
Said, 'Glad to see you like pot-pourri!'

The story spread, as did her fame
As Mrs Nutter – such a shame.
These days, when asked, she's never free –
A nervous social escapee;
And sits at home now, if you please,
With TV dinners on her knees.

The Golfer Who Was His Own Worst Opponent

Bob Kippax, it was widely known,
Preferred to play golf on his own.
He never, ever got depressed
Or, if he fluffed a short putt, stressed.
The great thing was, he'd always win.
No matter where they placed the pin,
Or what he scored by way of strokes,
He'd got the edge on other blokes.
And, what's more, liked to tell them so,
Propping the bar up, blow by blow.

His empty boasts began to grate,
And nasty rumours percolate –
Not least around the locker room
(And on the terrace, we presume),
That Bob was not what he appeared,
And well below the salt, one feared.

So, rather than incur a snub
And sharp expulsion from the club,
He took to playing after hours
When no one could deny his powers.

One evening, coming down the last,
When everywhere was overcast,
His second landed on the green –
The sweetest shot he'd ever seen.
A birdie followed, just like that,
And Bob, relieved, removed his hat,
And bowed to all the members, who
Had come outside to catch a view
Of one whose gifts they dared deny,
But now for which they'd surely die.

He bowed again, and waved, and beamed;
The lights behind the French doors gleamed.
He threw his fans a final glance ...
Then realised they were potted plants.

Up in the bar men shook their heads
As Bob slunk through the flowerbeds.
In golf clubs one's allowed to fail,
But lunacy's beyond the pale.

Now Bob plays at a pitch 'n' putt.
The club house is a wooden hut.
And no one cheers a hole in one
Where everyone is there for fun.

Drama Class

One thing we theatre-goers dread
Is finding that our neighbour's dead.
It seriously spoils one's evening so,
And makes one less inclined to go.

Giles Porringer, his ex-wife Jan,
Her sister and another man
Were sitting through a play by Shaw
When someone close began to snore.

The fellow in the seat in front
(For it was he) gave out a grunt.
His head went back, his jaw was slack –
The victim of a cardiac.

Some audience members sitting near
Began to shush and cough and peer.
The noise got worse, a nasty rattle
Like sabres in a Crimea battle
Now issued from his open maw.
Poor Giles thought, Cripes! He's dead for sure.

The man next door said, 'Hold my coat,
And push two fingers down his throat,
And grab his tongue. Don't let him choke.
One false move on your part, he'll croak.'

'Are you quite certain?' Giles hissed.
'I am a trained chiropodist,'
The man replied. 'A lucky chance.
I'm off to find an ambulance.'

And now a chilly silence falls
Across the stage, across the stalls,
As all the theatre longs to know
Which way this tragedy will go.

The lights go up and Giles is seen –
A most reluctant drama queen.

Two paramedics hurry through
With stretcher ready, right on cue.
They kneel down beside the stiff ...

Who clears his throat and gives a sniff,
And wakes out of a well-earned snooze
To find a total stranger who's
Got both his fingers down his gob,
While goggling like a halfwit knob.

'I've had enough of this!' he cried.
'Remove your hand and have some pride.
What is the theatre coming to?
It's worse than visiting the zoo.
It gives a decent chap the pip
Who cannot have an honest kip.'

Another moral for the list:
BEWARE ALL JOBS THAT END WITH -IST.

Cold Cuts

My in-laws came from Stourbridge
To see our brand-new house;
And all that I had in the fridge
Was cold, left-over grouse.

Déjà Vu in Oxford Street

Jack Huntsman had a rough divorce;
He thought his wife looked like a horse,
And told her so in unminced words,
And went off after younger birds.

While sauntering down Oxford Street
One day, a pair of dainty feet
Attracted his all-roving eye.
His heart leapt up, he gave a sigh –
Those shapely legs, that perky bum,
That swanlike neck, that shape, and some …

He followed her to Bond Street Tube
While softly humming the 'Blue Danube'.
She paused. He stopped. He cleared his throat.
He buttoned up his cashmere coat.
He said, 'I'm not a Peeping Tom,
But when I see a real bomb—'

She turned. The smile froze on her lips.
His mouth dried up, as did his quips.

She said, 'You've got a bloody cheek.
My boyfriend told me that last week.
He means it, and I think, What luck,
But from my erstwhile husband – Yuk!'

Old School Ties

Mike is an old Fentonian –
A decent sort of guy.
He'd rather be Etonian,
And wear an OE tie.

But who knows where the dice will fall?
Or how life will pan out?
To be at public school at all
You're better in than out.

His school career was not the best;
His work was borderline.
He never wore a First Eight vest,
But still he made Top Swine.

Long gone the days of Toggers Room,
Back Passage and New Squits,
And Double Jankers (words of doom),
And washing in The Pits.

As Top Swine, he was hung about
With privilege galore.
At Refec he walked in and out
Through Tommy Tiddles' Door.

And, best of all, a Swine could stroll
On Pegram's Piece, no less,
And sit about on Arthur's Hole
And eat a Fenton Mess.

One day, Mike, O.F., 43,
Interior Decorator,
Decided on a whim to see
His dear old Alma Mater.

He picked a sunny Saturday,
And drove down via Chatham.
He parked his car near Mincers Way,
And strolled through Apthorpe's Bottom.

He breathed the healthy Kentish air;
He'd never felt so happy
Since shaving Halfshaft's pubic hair
While wearing a large nappy.

On Pegram's Piece a man called out,
'No strangers on the grass!'
Mike said, 'You're right, I have no doubt.
You may think me an arse.

'In fact I am not what I seem;
I am an old Top Swine –
An honour, one might say the cream,
In ninety sixty-nine.

'As such I have the perfect right
To walk on Pegram's Piece,
And, if I wish, to fly a kite,
And drive a flock of geese.

'Tradition is what made this school;
Tradition's what made me;
Tradition here has been the rule
Since eighteen ninety-three.'

'Now look,' said his inquisitor,
'You may have been a toff,
But now you're just a visitor,
So kindly bugger off!'

Mike's still an Old Fentonian.
But wears an OE tie,
And claims he's an Etonian,
And no one blinks an eye.

Sally-Anne, Who Mistook
Herself for Mimi

The nation's keenest opera fan
Was Nico's cousin, Sally-Anne.
The Garden was her natural home;
Vienna, Paris, New York, Rome
Were other favourite stamping grounds
For wondrous sights and glorious sounds.
But, best of all, in summertime

There was no venue more sublime
Than Bogle Park in Gloucestershire,
Where opera's mounted *en plein air*.
She stayed with friends called Spencer-Gore,
Who owned the Rectory next door,
And after dinner every guest
Would stroll, immaculately dressed,
To where the most romantic tales
Competed with the nightingales.

One year the opera was *Bohème*;
The party list was much the same,
Except our heroine had a cough,
And would have called the whole thing off
(There's nothing like a few days' rest
When struggling with a nasty chest),
But couldn't bear to miss a note –
Or wear a nice warm overcoat ...

The evening turned out grey and cold,
But on the stage it was pure gold.
The show went well, with great applause,
Then everybody trooped indoors,
Where Sally-Anne popped straight to bed,
And, by the morning, was brown bread.

With opera, the gravest sin
Is thinking you're your heroine.

Lowlights

For people who are colour blind
Life must prove quite a challenge.
Gus dyed his greying hair to find
He's prematurely orange.

Parent Power

Orlando was a journalist –
A good one, even slightly pissed.
He wrote on food, and wine, and sport;
His expertise was often sought
For pieces needed in a hurry
By glossy weeklies based in Surrey.
He rightly prided his renown
For never letting any down.

So when his perky daughter, Fay,
Accosted him one sunny day
To ask if he would help her write
An essay about Chaucer's Knight,
He didn't hesitate, or blink;
He made his mind up in a wink.
Though way outside his expertise,
He reckoned he could always squeeze
A few words out of anything,
From Heisenberg to Wagner's *Ring*.
You don't need to be academic;
A writer's talent is endemic.

'Leave it to me!' He tapped his nose,
And wrote a page of peerless prose –
Professional, well wrought enough
To stand alongside his best stuff.
Fay changed the odd word here and there
To give it a more youthful air,
And sweetly pecked him on the cheek,
And took it into school that week ...

When children's brains begin to slump,
It's all hands to the homework pump.
A quick leg-up is all they need
To help them get back up to speed.
Their gratitude is plain to see –
Though not when Dad gets them a D.

A La Recherche du Feather Boa

Sir Edward Tooley was the sort
Whose marriages were somewhat fraught.
At twenty-three he'd married Rayne,
But met a woman on a train,
Who'd given him a knowing glance
And whisked him to the South of France.

He married her, became a pa
And lived in St-Jean-Cap-Ferrat
For several years until he fell
In love with the exotic Belle –
A dancer at the Crazy Horse,
Who showed him lots of tricks, of course,
Including one with feather boas –
A practice known to real goers
Who swing this way (and sometimes that),
And often do it in a hat.

A marriage of full-on delight
Concluded when she saw the light
With Mrs Pike, became her slave,
And changed her name from Belle to Dave.

Now Ted was a quixotic bloke,
But this behaviour made him choke.
He felt there must be better ways
Of spending his maturer days
Than wasting time with women, who
Quite clearly hadn't got a clue
That underneath that waggish head
There lay a sober, serious Ted.

He wondered if he ever would
Meet someone who was kind and good.

But then at last he settled down
With dumpy, frumpy Margaret Brown,
A tour guide with the National Trust,
And owner of a queen-size bust,
Who, in her battered panama,
Looked oddly like his dear mama.

They lived for many years in Kent,
In Tenterden, in deep content.
With horses and assorted pets,
Adopted from the local vet's,
Among them Jack, the Border terrier;
As Margaret said, 'The more the merrier.'

Sir Edward joined the local choir,
Raised money for the old church spire,
And organised the village fete,
And holidayed in Bassenthwaite –
A figure in the neighbourhood,
A paragon of all that's good.

Dear Margaret was the perfect wife;
She guaranteed the perfect life.
She pandered to his every whim,
And never, ever bothered him.

And yet, for all her gentle ways,
He thought back to the good old days
Of sexy Belle and Cap-Ferrat,
Of wine and song and brouhaha,
And midnight swims with real goers,
And fun and games and feather boas.

The more his wife began to waddle,
The more he thought, A younger model
Is what a man of sixty needs –
And long blonde hair, and rings, and beads.

'I'm leaving you,' he told poor Meg.
'You'll think I am a rotten egg,
But really it is for the best.
There, now I've got that off my chest.'

She looked at him with pitying eyes.
'I think you're being very wise.
I'm leaving too and, furthermore,
The man I love is thirty-four.

'He's not the slightest bit like you;
He's got a funny mother, who
I'm told is quite a racy type
Who wears men's clothes and smokes a pipe.

'She's quite old now and lives in France.
I gather she once used to dance,
And mixed with what you might call goers,
And did strange things with feather boas.'

Now Edward lives with scruffy Jack,
Whose hair is thinning down his back;
But never mind, he's young at heart,
And, as dogs go, he's pretty smart.
The pair have moved to old Genoa,
Where people say Jack's quite a goer.

Back Story

Horatio's mother was no sage,
But on the subject of old age
Her talk was full of *bon*-ish *mots*,
And mental tappings on the nose.
'Don't bother to grow old, my dear;
There is no future there, I fear'
Was one she often liked to air,
Descending in her favourite chair
Amid the usual grunts ands groans
And puffs and pants and creaking bones.

Now Hozza's getting on himself,
And feeling slightly on the shelf,
Thanks largely to a painful back,
Which seems to baffle quack on quack.
And courses of manipulation,
Lashings of warm embrocation,
Swimming in the local lido
(Wearing quite a nasty Speedo) –
Nothing eased the non-stop tweak
Day on day and week on week.

A friend, Sid Eddis, had a wheeze:
Once in the Outer Hebrides
He'd skydived with a family friend –
'It's something I could recommend.
To free-fall through the air's one thing
With all the thrills that that can bring.
It's better than a superdrug.
But when you give the cord a tug,
It deals your system quite a jolt,
As if struck by a massive volt.
Now that might take your pain away
By stretching out your vertebrae.'

Horatio was a pragmatist
(And, not to say, empiricist).
His favourite maxim was 'Needs must',
To which he liked to add 'or bust'.
As treatments go, this seemed plain dotty,
But when a chap is going potty,
He'll clutch at any passing straw,
Or make for any open door –
Albeit at five thousand feet,
Connected to a man called Pete,
Who said, 'Just leave it all to me.
Relax, enjoy yourself, feel free
To wave your arms and scream and shout.
Up here there's no one else about.'

With that he launched them into space,
Like Victory over Samothrace.
Their arms spread wide, they plunged to earth,
And Hozza wondered, Is it worth
This trouble for a dodgy back?
And at that very moment – thwack!
The chute flew out. 'Geronimo!'
He shouted. 'Crikey! Here we go!'

The pain had flown. Like thistledown,
They floated oh so gently down,
And landed like two butterflies.
He couldn't quite believe his eyes
That he was safe back home again,
And, what's more, free at last from pain.

His parachute lay on the ground;
His friends and family gathered round.
He said, 'I've never felt so good
In all my life since childhood!'
He turned to give a hug to Pete;
His chute strings tangled round his feet;
He stumbled, took a backward trip,
Fell on his side and broke his hip.

When doing something new, do try,
To walk before you learn to fly.

Gastroshambles

Miranda is a brilliant cook,
But never does things by the book.
She improvises in a trice;
She'll chop and dice and chuck in spice,
And never gets caught on the hop,
Or dishes up a total flop.

But Lady Luck can be so cruel
And turn a great dish into gruel,
As happened just the other day,
When Ben's best friend, Sam, came to play.

'I'll give them supper,' she agreed.
There really wasn't any need
To go to town for two small boys,
Whose tastes for electronic toys,
Outweighed those for gastronomy
At supper, breakfast, lunch and tea.

She found some frozen mince. Of course!
Some meatballs in a pesto sauce
Should satisfy their inner men
And make sure Sam stays friends with Ben,

She fried them in a tick – hey presto!
And then disaster struck: no pesto!

She quickly made a sauce with cheese –
A standby that would surely please –
But felt she really must explain,
If only to assuage her pain.

Young Sam's face fell; he looked quite glum.
'No pesto!' he exclaimed. 'My mum
Puts pesto into everything.
Oh, dear; that's quite embarrassing.'

He ate the balls, but left the sauce:
It should have been Gruyère. Of course.

Now Ben's best friend's a boy called Pips,
Whose favourite food is egg and chips.
He eats Miranda's food and smiles,
And thinks she's the best cook by miles.

Putting on the Ritz

Young Harry is a journalist –
A travel-writing specialist.
While all his friends have full-time jobs,
He's satisfied with bits and bobs.
The freelance lifestyle suits him best;
Unlike his pals, he's never stressed.
With itchy feet, devoid of strings,
He loves the freedom travel brings.

And, more than that, he loves the fact
That others are so hugely hacked
That, unlike them, without a care,
He lives just like a millionaire
At other people's kind expense
For, frankly, little recompense,
Beyond a glowing piece or two,
Directed at the well-to-do.

He often travels in first class,
And treats his well-dressed, well-fed arse
To five-star luxury and more,
And mingles with the topmost drawer
From St Tropez to Angkor Wat,
And Necker Island on a yacht.
He acts the *crème*-ist *de la crème*
So well, they think he's one of them,
And drops names with a careless ease
Like garments in a cheap striptease.

Once, staying with fiancée, Sue,
He showed off to her parents, too –
The Hendersons in Potters Bar,
Who never ventured very far,
Or found themselves in hotels where
The customers routinely dare
To pilfer everything in sight,
Assuming that it is their right.

But Harry, anxious to impress,
With talk of every good address,
Held forth at lunch with travellers' tales
From Rajasthan to New South Wales,
Oblivious to their stifled yawns
Over the Marie Rose-dressed prawns.

That evening, as they met for drinks,
His hostess said amid the chinks,
'I do hope you don't mind, but I
Went in your room to cast an eye
And check that you've got everything –
A towel, some soap, that kind of thing.
But I see you've come well supplied.'

At that young Harry nearly died.
He'd unpacked earlier in haste,
And not the slightest bit shamefaced.
The contents of his Antler bag
Were scattered round, with all the swag
He'd nicked from myriad posh hotels,
Hand towels and unguents, shower gels,
An ashtray, slippers, flannel mitts,
A fluffy bathrobe from the Ritz ...
With all their famous names displayed,
And every one of them top grade.

Though nothing more was said, it's true,
By Mrs H, he knew they knew.

The Frame Alone ...

The sharpest connoisseurs in town
Were Bill and Barbara Muspratt-Brown.
They specialised in British art;
They were not rich, but they were smart.
Habitués at private views,
They were the first to hear the news
Of who was buying what and where,
From Tring to Weston-super-Mare.
Both Friends of the Academy,
They were the pure epitome
Of art historians *manqués*,
Who know their stuff and what to say,
And fill their walls with frightful tosh –
Quite nice, but basically eyewash.

Babs dreamed of finding something great –
A painting worthy of the Tate,
Which would enhance their social stature,
And be a pension for the future –
One they could pick up for a song.
As experts, they could not go wrong.

'Fat chance,' said Bill. 'And pigs might fly,'
And added words like 'pie' and 'sky'.

But Fate is always lurking near
To catch you one behind the ear,
And Bill was well and truly floored
When, seated at his clavichord,
Babs marched in looking pleased as Punch,
At half-past twelve, in time for lunch,
Clutching a large plastic bag,
Just like a burglar with his swag.
'I've dreamed of something valuable,
And bought a little Constable
For twenty quid, not bad at all.
I found it on a market stall,'
She said. Bill, like a halibut, just goggled;
His pulse rate soared, his brain fair boggled.
She took it out. He said, 'By gum,
I think you've hit the jackpot, chum!
A *Study of the River Stour*!
In my view we could well insure
It for a hundred thou, at least.
In art I am no *arriviste*.
I know a Constable when I see one,
And I've no doubt that this could be one.
There's only one way to find out –
Give a top auction room a shout.
They'll want to see it straight away.
Get onto one without delay!'

The nice Bond Street receptionist
Was clearly not a specialist.
'I'll get someone to have a look.'
She took it to a little nook
Behind the desk and made a call –
'Could you, please, come down to the hall?
A lady has a Constable;
She thinks it might be valuable.'

A nice young man in pinstripe suit,
Who oozed good manners and repute,
Appeared and said, 'What have we here?
An English scene, it would appear.
A Study of the River Stour.
It's very neatly done, I'm sure.
But could it be the real McCoy?
Is this a lost piece by our boy?'

He hummed and hahed and coughed and sniffed,
Like one presented with a gift
Of two small eggs by Fabergé,
Who doesn't know quite what to say.

'I must admit,' he said at last,
'I've seen some copies in the past,
And to be frank, as copies go,
In my opinion this rates low.
With luck it might make fifty quid –
I doubt, though, if you'd get a bid.'

Now Barbara has a steady head,
But anybody would see red
Whose future life goes up in smoke,
Courtesy of some snooty bloke.

Poor Babs was absolutely thrown –
'*Just fifty?* But the frame alone ...!'

The suit said, 'Let's not be verbose;
For me it verges on the gross.'

Still through the building came this moan –
'The frame alone …! The frame alone …!'

And now it hangs there on their wall,
And Babs reveals to one and all:
'Our little sketch by Constable.
Yes, I would say it's valuable.'

Bullitt

Now Roddy never went as far
As owning an exotic car.
The sportiest job he ever drove
(A clapped-out Triumph, painted mauve)
Was not the type to turn girls' heads,
Or get them jumping into beds.
A failed Clarkson through and through,
He raced a friend to Timbuktu,
But broke down in torrential rain
Outside a bar in northern Spain.

But still at heart a petrol-head,
His first move as a newly-wed
Was taking Liz to Silverstone –
The dullest day she'd ever known.

When he became a family man,
He bought a boring camper van –
An old converted Vivaro.
'A little dull, but it can go,'
He told his muckers in the pub.
He didn't want to risk a snub.

One day, while driving back from Slough,
He had the chance to show just how.
A Panda came up close behind,
And Roddy, thinking to be kind
And pull in so the chaps could pass,
Accelerated, like an arse,
To find the inside lane was full,
Like rush hour in Old Istanbul.

He couldn't find the tiniest gap
And got into a frightful flap
As on and on and on he flew,
Tailgated by the boys in blue,
Until his scramble for a place
Had turned into a full car chase.

They pulled him in near Baron's Court.
'I hate to be a spoilsport,'
Said one, 'You may be Stirling Moss,
But, frankly, I don't give a toss.
My name is PC Benedict,
And you are well and truly nicked.'

These days Rod rides a Boris bike
And, being ever sportsmanlike,
On early mornings, in the dark,
On pavements, crossings, in the park,
He'll never try to use his brake
If there's a chance to overtake.

Foot in Mouth Outbreak

Will Baskerville is twenty-eight
And rising through the ranks:
The sort of would-be heavyweight
Who flourishes in banks.

His pretty wife, called Anne-Marie,
Is also doing well.
She sells exotic pot-pourri
To well-heeled clientele.

The office party is the time
When young men like to shine,
And chaps like Will, who hope to climb,
Go easy on the wine.

So when his boss stepped in the lift
With wife in evening dress,
This had to be the perfect gift
For William to impress.

Now Tim, his boss, is fifty-four,
But those who meet him say
He could be thirty-five, no more –
A modern Dorian Gray.

His wife's the same age, give or take,
And looks exactly that:
A feisty woman, no mistake –
Quite small and slightly fat.

'My wife Penelope,' said Tim.
'This is our young star, Phil.'
Will shook her hand, and smiled at him.
'Some people call me Will.'

He waved a paw at Anne-Marie,
'And this is *my* mother,' he said.
He goggled at the other three
And promptly turned bright red.

His boss said, 'Nice to meet you, mum.
You're looking very well –
Unlike your son who's been struck dumb.
So ... hail and farewell!'

There are certain situations
When you're fairly bang to rights.
Accept humiliations;
Save your strength for other fights.

A Word in Your Shell-Like

Men with the wrong shoes
May not be welcomed into
Polite society.

Red Trousers in Regatta Shock

Ned's trousers were red corduroy;
He wore a silk cravat;
One step above the hoi-polloi –
An ocean-going prat.
He sometimes sported purple trews,
And claimed to be a Scot.
His matching face was bright with booze,
His chit-chat utter rot.

A serious weekender,
He'd join the piss-head bunch –
A practised elbow-bender,
Well rat-arsed before lunch.

And, being quite oblivious
To those not in his set,
His conduct could prove bilious
To others that he met.

His voice was loud and booming;
It had a nasal drawl.
His presence, large and looming,
Was guaranteed to pall.

As for his ghastly bright red cords
(Unheeded by his chums),
They'd win the National Twat Awards
On far less outsize bums.

One day he met his Waterloo
At Henley, of all places,
When all the usual drinking crew
Rolled up with purple faces.

The oarsmen strained and bent their backs;
The men in pink caps roared;
But for these dipsomaniacs
The racing was ignored.

They lowered pint on pint of Pimm's,
Scoffed lobster, quaffed champagne,
And chanted silly made-up hymns;
Their jokes got more inane.

They partied on, the sky turned black
And, not to be outdone,
Some local rowdies in a pack
Turned up to spoil their fun.

It wasn't all Ned's fault, as such;
When nature called, he went.
He really couldn't see that much
Behind the nearby tent.

The Asbo, halfway through his smoke
Was feeling pretty rotten,
When suddenly this hooray bloke
Peed on his track-suit bottom.

Ned might have got away with it
By lobbing him some dough,
But, ever the red-trousered twit,
He told him where to go.

The two best sights that year, beside
The Maggie's Discotheque,
Was some man floating on the tide,
His red cords round his neck.

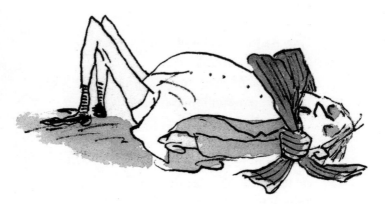